TO

Alan Schmitt
2018

The Other Side of Psalm 23

ALAN SCHMITT

Copyright © 2018 Alan Schmitt.

All rights reserved. No part of this book may be used or reproduced by any means, graphic, electronic, or mechanical, including photocopying, recording, taping or by any information storage retrieval system without the written permission of the author except in the case of brief quotations embodied in critical articles and reviews.

WestBow Press books may be ordered through booksellers or by contacting:

WestBow Press
A Division of Thomas Nelson & Zondervan
1663 Liberty Drive
Bloomington, IN 47403
www.westbowpress.com
1 (866) 928-1240

Because of the dynamic nature of the Internet, any web addresses or links contained in this book may have changed since publication and may no longer be valid. The views expressed in this work are solely those of the author and do not necessarily reflect the views of the publisher, and the publisher hereby disclaims any responsibility for them.

Any people depicted in stock imagery provided by Getty Images are models, and such images are being used for illustrative purposes only. Certain stock imagery © Getty Images.

ISBN: 978-1-9736-2460-8 (sc)
ISBN: 978-1-9736-2459-2 (e)

Print information available on the last page.

WestBow Press rev. date: 3/30/2018

NIV: All Scripture quotations, unless otherwise indicated, are taken from the Holy Bible, New International Version®, NIV®. Copyright ©1973, 1978, 1984, 2011 by Biblica, Inc.™ Used by permission of Zondervan. All rights reserved worldwide. www.zondervan.com The "NIV" and "New International Version" are trademarks registered in the United States Patent and Trademark Office by Biblica, Inc.

CEV: Scripture quotations marked (CEV) are from the Contemporary English Version Copyright © 1991, 1992, 1995 by American Bible Society. Used by Permission.

CBV: Scripture taken from the Cloverdale Bible

JCB: aken from the Complete Jewish Bible by David H. Stern. Copyright © 1998. All rights reserved. Used by permission of Messianic Jewish Publishers, 6120 Day Long Lane, Clarksville, MD 21029. www.messianicjewish.net.

GBV: Scripture taken from the Geneva Bible

DRA (Douay-Rheims Bible): Scripture taken from the Douay-Rheims Bible

KJV: Scripture taken from the King James Version of the Bible

NKJV: Scripture taken from the New King James Version®. Copyright © 1982 by Thomas Nelson. Used by permission. All rights reserved.

ERV (Easy to read version): License Agreement for Bible Texts World Bible Translation Center Last Updated: July 27, 2001 Copyright © 2001 by World Bible Translation Center All rights reserved.

NRSV: Scripture quotations are from New Revised Standard Version Bible, copyright © 1989 National Council of the Churches of Christ in the United States of America. Used by permission. All rights reserved.

TLB (Living Bible): Scripture quotations marked (TLB) are taken from The Living Bible copyright © 1971. Used by permission of Tyndale House Publishers, Inc., Carol Stream, Illinois 60188. All rights reserved.

NLT: Scripture quotations marked (NLT) are taken from the Holy Bible, New Living Translation, copyright ©1996, 2004, 2015 by Tyndale House Foundation. Used by permission of Tyndale House Publishers, Inc., Carol Stream, Illinois 60188. All rights reserved.

MSG: Scripture quotations marked MSG are taken from THE MESSAGE, copyright © 1993, 1994, 1995, 1996, 2000, 2001, 2002 by Eugene H. Peterson. Used by permission of NavPress. All rights reserved. Represented by Tyndale House Publishers, Inc.

Contents

Preface: Why write another book about
      Psalm 23?...xi

Chapter 1: Why Sheep and Shepherds?.................1
Chapter 2: The Sheep and the Shepherd............12
Chapter 3: Green Pastures and Still Waters.......21
Chapter 4: Help! I've fallen and I can't get up!....33
Chapter 5: The Tools of the Trade....................45
Chapter 6: Tables and Valleys 57
Chapter 7: What is a Shepherd Church?............65

Epilogue..75
Bible References 79

Foreword

I had the pleasure of meeting Dr. Alan Schmitt when he became a student, and a graduate of my bible college. My introduction to Dr. Schmitt was a meeting set up by the Lord! I found him to be a scholar already when he joined the college. I was so impressed he is now a board member of this worldwide college.

His book is not just for a funeral you go to. He digs deep in a profound and understandable way into the riches of Psalms 23. The reader of this book will never look at Psalms 23 the same again. I was blessed while reading the manuscript.

Everyone needs to learn that the Lord is our Shepherd and our provider while we are living. The book explains the living, vibrant life a Christian can have by grasping the concepts of the relationship of the shepherd and his sheep.

Do not wait until you have to go to a funeral to read the riches explained by Dr. Schmitt in Psalms 23. This is a book you will want to pass on to others.

Dr. Danny Abaldo, Founder, Dean, and Head Professor
Truth and Mercy Institute for Advanced Ministry Studies
Yermo, CA

Preface

Pathos.com is a non-denominational, non-partisan online destination site that seeks to provide a platform for a global dialogue about religion and spirituality, and to explore and experience the world's beliefs.

According to an article published in their onling blog, the *Christian Crier*, May of 2015, of the top seven scriptures most read, studied, and written about, Psalm 23:1-6 (the 23rd Psalm) comes in third following John 3:16 and Matthew 6:9-13 (the Lord's Prayer).[1]

Considering the thousands of books, articles, essays, study guides, and theological dissertations that have been written and published over the years, why another one about Psalm 23?

That's what I thought, until I discovered one such book entitled: *A Shepherd Looks at Psalm 23*, published in 2007 by the late W. Phillip Keller. In 144 short pages, Keller gave me insights into Psalm 23 that illuminated the words of David in ways I had never understood before. After some sixty years of being a student of the Bible, forty of which I served as a local pastor, that was exciting!

Whenever I have gained new insights into scripture, my first reaction as a pastor has been the desire to share those insights with others. Such was the case with the work of Mr. Keller. In 2015, I incorporated the insights I gained from his perspective on Psalm 23 into a series of sermons I called, *The Other Side of Psalm 23*. In 2018, my doctoral dissertation was based on those sermons. Today, they are presented in this book for your review and consideration.

I have prefaced each chapter with a reading of Psalm 23:1-6 from different translations or paraphrase of the Bible. I encourage you to read each one of them out loud before beginning the chapter text.

It is my hope and prayer that because the Lord truly is your shepherd, you will be empowered and encouraged by the unconditional love of God to live your life secure in the presence of the Lord today, tomorrow, and forever. Amen!

Thank You

No one writes a book alone. Most of the printed words may come from the one whose name appears on the cover. But the inspiration, insights, and experiences that produce those printed words come from a wonderful circle of family, friends, colleagues, and all those unnamed or forgotten saints that God so graciously plants along our life journey. This book is no exception.

To those who have been a source of inspiration to me, those who have graciously shared their insights with me, and to those whose experiences have illuminated the path of my life journey, I say Thank You!

Thank You to Dr. Danny L. Abaldo, Founder and Professor of Truth and Mercy Institute of Advanced Ministry Studies, for his commitment to training pastors and Christian leaders throughout the world. His friendship, wisdom, and words of encouragement have been invaluable.

Thank You to the late W. Phillip Keller (1920-1997), photographer, agronomist, and author of over thirty-five books on Christian subjects, including his most popular book *A Shepherd Looks at Psalm 23*. The insights I gained from his work have been the springboard for this publication.

Thank You to those who have devoted many hours to reading my words, proofing my words, and offering invaluable advice and counsel regarding how I could better put my words together.

While on the References page I have attempted to give credit to specific works I have used in my Psalm 23 journey, I accept the reality that time and fading memory have inadvertently caused me to forget others. To all who may fall into this category, I say Thank You!

Finally, I offer my eternal gratitude to the gracious God who has bestowed on me the honor of using my words, to speak His Word.

In the name of the Father, and of the Son, and of the Holy Spirit: Amen!

Alan Schmitt, DMin
2018

One

Why Sheep and Shepherds?

The Coverdale Bible, compiled by Myles Coverdale and published in 1535, was the first complete Modern English translation of the Bible.

> Psalm 23:1-6 *"The Lord is my shepherd therefore can I lack nothing. He shall feed me in a green pasture and lead me forth beside the waters of comfort. He shall convert my soul and bring me forth in the paths of righteousness, for his Name's sake. Yea, though I walk through the valley of the shadow of death, I will fear no evil for thou art with me; thy rod and thy staff comfort me. Thou shalt prepare a table before me against them that trouble me thou hast anointed my head with oil, and my cup shall be full. But thy loving-kindness and mercy shall follow me*

Alan Schmitt

> *all the days of my life and I will dwell in the house of the Lord forever."* (CBV)

Three hymns. Three recognizable hymns. Three classic hymns. Three hymns that have one thing in common. See if you can pick it out.

"I come to the garden alone While the dew is still on the roses and the voice I hear, falling on my ear The Son of God discloses And He walks with me And He talks with me And He tells me I am His own And the joy we share as we tarry there None other has ever known." [2]

"There let the way appear, Steps unto heav'n; All that thou sendest me, In mercy giv'n; Angels to beckon me Nearer, my God, to thee, Nearer, my God, to thee, Nearer to thee!" [3]

"Should you go first and I remain to walk the road alone I'll live in memory's garden dear with happy days we've known In spring I'll wait for roses red, when fades the lilacs bloom And in early fall when brown leaves fall, I'll catch a glimpse of you." [4]

Did you catch it? They are all funeral songs. Songs that are rarely sung any place or any time other than at funerals or memorial services. *In the Garden,* was written by C, Austin Miles in 1912; *Nearer My God to Thee,* was written by Sarah

Flower Adams in 1841; *Beyond the Sunset*, was written by Virgil P. Brock in 1936.

Three beautiful songs celebrating the blessed assurance of eternity that are by their traditional application restricted to times of sorrow and mourning: funerals and memorial services. Three songs that are rarely sung in Sunday morning worship. When was the last time you were in church and heard the worship leader say: "Please remain standing for our hymn of celebration: Beyond the Sunset?"

One of my favorite songs that is occasionally sung in worship, is another example of a funeral song: "The Old Rugged Cross." I love that Song! It conveys a powerful message of God's unconditional love. But every time I sing it, I have a visual flashback to my dad laying in a casket at the front of the chapel of Theme Funeral Home on Boonville St., in Springfield, MO, some 55 years ago.

Listen to portions of three familiar scriptures. Same question: What do they all have in common?

John 14:1-4: *"Do not let your hearts be troubled. You believe in God; believe also in me. My Father's house has many rooms; if that were not so, would I have told you that I am going there to prepare a place for you? And if I go and prepare a place for you, I will come back and take you to be with me that you also may be where I am."* (NIV)

Corinthians 5:1: *"For we know that if the earthly tent we live in is destroyed, we have a building from God, an eternal house in heaven, not built by human hands."* (NIV)

<u>Psalm 23:1:</u> *"The LORD is my shepherd; I shall not want..."* (NKJV)

What do they all have in common? They are all funeral scriptures. Scriptures that are seldom read any place or any other time other than at funerals or memorial services. I think in many ways that's regrettable.

I will be the first to acknowledge their time-tested ability to soften the sting of death and provide comforting words of hope and assurance. I have witnessed firsthand how they can sooth the pain of loss and loneliness when someone we love has been taken away from us. On the other hand, it seems to me that their being exclusively consigned to funerals or memorial services precludes the greater illumination of the divine truths they contain.

A case in point is Psalm 23. It is by far the most recognized bereavement passage of scripture in the Bible to both believers and non-believers alike. Its use in worship liturgy and litanies is second in popularity only to the Lord's Prayer. I will confess to you that I am guilty-as-charged when it comes to limiting the use of Psalm 23 to funerals and memorial services.

Since 1972, when I was appointed to my first church, I have officiated at forty funerals and memorial services. Yes, I have kept a record. I have lead services ranging from a still-born infant to a

The Other Side of Psalm 23

99-year-old saint. I have presided over services for those who have died long and agonizing deaths, those who have died suddenly, and one young lady who took her own life. With only a few exceptions, Psalm 23 has been the anchor passage of scripture I have relied on. Chances are, I will continue to incorporate it into the litany of services I am invited to lead. That's okay.

The bereavement side of Psalm 23 is important and necessary as long as we realize that there is another side to 23. As one writer has put it: "No single psalm has expressed more powerfully man's prayer of confidence to the God whose purpose alone gives meaning to the span of life, from womb to tomb." [5]

Psalm 23 is a psalm of life. "(It) functions to remind its audience of the relationship between God and God's people and, perhaps most importantly, the psalm reminds readers about the beauties of living life in the here and now even amid the usual darkness that accompanies day-to-day life."[12] In six verses, 117 words, we are given the undeniable assurance of the provision and protection our shepherd provides for us as we walk through the valley and the shadow of life. With that in mind, I want to invite you travel with me as we explore the *Other Side of Psalm 23*.

Let's begin our journey by taking a brief side trip back to a time known as the English Reformation. The pigeonholing of Psalm 23 into a litany reserved for only funerals or memorial services can be traced back to three things that happened in England in the mid to late 1500's.

1. In 1534, the English domination by the Catholic Church and the supremacy of the pope over the lives of British subjects was officially rejected. In its place, the Church of England was established and was declared to be the only legitimate and sanctioned religious expression in all of Great Britain.

2. In 1547, every local church in England was required to have a copy of the whole Bible in English. This access to the scripture in the common vernacular of the people was designed to restrict or eliminate the early Catholic practice of misinterpreting scripture to support the Papal agenda. The first "authorized" English translation of the Bible was the Coverdale Bible, compiled by Bishop Myles Coverdale in 1535.

3. In 1549, there appeared the first edition of the *Book of Common Prayer*. It was designed as a means to standardize the liturgies and litanies of worship used in each local church. It included morning prayers and evening prayers, along with prescribed orders of worship for Sunday services, Holy Communion, Baptism, Confirmation, Marriage, and the burial of the dead.

In the orders for the burial of the dead, the recitation of Psalm 23 was established as the primary anchor passage of scripture for funeral and

The Other Side of Psalm 23

memorial services. It was the Book of Common Prayer that caused Psalm 23:1-6 to become simply the Twenty-Third Psalm.

Why sheep and shepherds? Answer: *Similitudes*. Finding and using common, understandable points of reference, with which to compare the unknown to the known. In particular, the common practice of assigning names, descriptions, traits, or characteristics to the unknown of the divine that has a known human counterpart; a real-life comparison; a point of reference.

In modern literature, similitudes are sometimes referred to as analogy, metaphor, illustration, or simile. Biblical similitude clue words and phrases are *likeness*, *image*, or *is like*. The kingdom of heaven parables taught by Jesus used similitudes. The kingdom of heaven *is like* a hidden treasure; *is like* a tiny mustard seed; *is like* a determined woman looking for her lost coin; *is like* a barren fig tree; is like a pearl of great price: all examples of word pictures that illustrate the unknown, by using the known.

The first example of a similitude in scripture is found in Genesis 1:26-27: *"Then God said, "Let us make man in our image, in our likeness... So, God created man in his own image, in the image of God he created him;"* Did you catch that? In their attempt to understand the divine unknown *(God)*, the writer of Genesis uses the description, traits, and characteristics of the known *(Man)*. God now has a body, and by cultural implication, a gender; God is a *he*.

Because he is a he and has the ability to create other he's and she's, he takes on the similitude of God the *father*. The unknown of God now takes on the known traits and characteristics of a loving father. A loving father who provides provision and protection for his children. If he is father, then his people are assigned the similitude of *children*; the children of God.

The gospels employ the similitude of *son* in describing who Jesus is. Jesus is the Son of God. He is the loving son of the loving father God. John 15:9: *"As the Father has loved me, so have I loved you."* He is a son who was just like his daddy. That must explain why Jesus refers to God as his Abba father 165 times in the Gospels. Abba is Aramaic and is best translated into English as *papa* or *daddy*.

Have I lost you yet? Any of you asking what does all of this have to do with sheep and shepherds? Think about this. If your goal is to explain the transcendent, creative, and sustaining omnipotent, omniscient, and omnipresent force in the universe, doesn't it make sense that you would seek out similitudes that are most familiar with the most people?

If the similitude of father is the obvious first choice, then a review of scripture quickly identifies the similitude of sheep and shepherds as second in importance. Why sheep and shepherds?

1. The economy of ancient Palestine was rooted in sheep and shepherds. The earliest record of occupations recorded in the Bible was raising sheep and farming. Genesis 4:2: *"Now Abel kept flocks, and Cain worked the soil."* Many of the early Biblical who's-who were shepherds who lived a nomadic lifestyle. Abraham, Lot, Isaac, Jacob, Rachel, Laban, Jacob's twelve sons, Moses, David, and Amos were all shepherds.

Nomads lived in tents and traveled from location to location, which was not very conducive to long term farming. So, sheep and shepherding became the primary economic base of early Palestine. Sheep became the primary source of food, milk to drink, wool for the weaving of cloth, even an early type of canvas used as covering material for tents. In Exodus 25, Moses specifies that rams skin dyed red are to be used as covering for the Tabernacle, which was the portable place of worship during the Exodus from Egypt.

Sheep skins were used for carrying food reserves such as grains and dried fruits and were used in the process of fermenting of wine. When yeast was introduced to the grape juice, it would transform the sugars into ethanol and carbon dioxide, which would cause the sheep skins to expand. When the fermentation process was complete, the sheepskin would harden. A kind of sheep skin box of wine. If you put new wine in old wineskins, the hardened skin would eventually burst and the wine would be lost.

In Mark 2:22, Jesus used the similitude of the wine skins to teach that it was impossible to mingle together the spiritual freedom of the gospel (new wine) with the old ceremonies of the Law (old wine skins). The horns of rams were used as musical instruments. They were called a shophar.

Sheep were a key element in Old Testament covenants. The most common seal of civil covenants, royal covenants, and divine covenants, was the letting of blood. In all three forms of covenant, the sacrificial animal of choice was a sheep. Common Old Testament practice was to cut sheep in half and the two parties walk between the halves. Origin of the phrase: "To cut a deal." Sheep were one of the common offerings in the Jewish sacrificial system. They were offered as burnt offerings, sin offerings, guilt offerings, and peace offerings.

2. If everyone was familiar with the importance of sheep to their economy, then doesn't it make sense that they would also be familiar with the nature of sheep and the role and relationship of the shepherd and their sheep? You suppose that is why the relationship between the sheep and the shepherd permeates the Biblical testimony of the relationship between God and his people? The role and relationship of sheep and shepherds is referenced over 200 times in scripture. You suppose that is why David began a psalm affirming the provision and

protection of God with the phrase: The Lord is my shepherd?

The nature of sheep and a closer look at the role and relationship of the shepherd and their sheep is where we will begin in Chapter 2.

Two

The Sheep and the Shepherd

The Complete Jewish Bible was translated by David H. Stern, an Israel-based Messianic Jewish theologian, 1998. The Old Testament is a paraphrase of the 1917 Jewish Publication Society version of the Tanakh (also known as the Masoretic Text).

> Psalm 23:1-6: *"Yahweh is my shepherd; I lack nothing. He has me lie down in grassy pastures, He leads me by quiet water, He restores my inner person. He guides me in right paths for the sake of his own name. Even if I pass through death-dark ravines, I will fear no disaster; for you are with me; your rod and staff reassure me. You prepare a table for me, even as my enemies watch; you anoint my head with oil from an overflowing cup. Goodness and*

grace will pursue me every day of my life; and I will live in the house of Yahweh for years and years to come." (JCB)

Move over Darwin and take your monkeys with you. According to the Bible, humans are more like sheep than any other animal.

The two-fold goal of Chapter 2 is: 1) Take a brief look at the generic nature of sheep. 2) Begin to illuminate the other side of Psalm 23 from the perspective of the relationship between the sheep and the shepherd, and frame it in a portrait of the relationship between God and his people.

1) Let's begin with a quick review of sheep 101 for all us city folks:

1. Sheep are over one year of age. Lambs are less than one year of age.

2. A female sheep is called an ewe.

3. A male sheep is called a ram.

4. A group of sheep is called a flock. Larger groups of sheep are called mobs.

5. A shepherd is the person who is ultimately responsible for the provision and protection of the sheep, because the sheep are incapable of providing for their own provision and protection.

That may be why writer, blogger, and Pastor Tim Challies has suggested the three characteristics of sheep are, "dumb, dependent, and defenseless." [6] As I understand the basic nature of sheep, I would like to describe them as followers, flockers, and fleers.

1. <u>Sheep are Followers:</u> Sheep will instinctively follow the sheep in front of them. Where one sheep goes, the rest of the flock will likely follow. Some call it the, *everywhere that Mary went, the lamb was sure to go* syndrome. A number of years ago, I read an article entitled: *450 sheep jump to their deaths in Turkey.*

"First one sheep jumped to its death. Then stunned Turkish shepherds, who had left the herd to graze while they had breakfast, watched as nearly 1,500 others followed, each leaping off the same cliff. In the end, 450 dead animals lay on top of one another in a billowy white pile. Those who jumped later were saved as the pile got higher and the fall more cushioned." [7]

If one sheep jumps over a cliff, the others are likely to follow. Hmm! So that's where my mom got that? Remember that one? "If your friends jump off a cliff, will you follow them?"

2. <u>Sheep are Flockers:</u> Sheep have a strong herding or flocking instinct. They are a social animal. When grazing, they need to see other sheep. Making sure that sheep always have visual contact with other sheep will reduce stress when moving or handling them.

According to animal behaviorists, "a group of five sheep is usually necessary for sheep to display their normal flocking behavior. A sheep will become

The Other Side of Psalm 23

highly agitated if it is separated from the rest of the flock."[13] You suppose that is where we get the idiom, *There is strength in numbers?*

1) A sheep will remain in a particular flock even if they don't necessarily get along with one or more of the other sheep in the group.

2) It takes a while for the sheep in a flock to accept a new sheep that is introduced to the group. When a new sheep arrives in the flock, the others will treat them as strangers, and force them to earn their spot in the group.

3) In addition to their need for visual contact with others in the group, sheep feel most calm and secure when they are touching other sheep.

4) While their instinct for flocking is strong, sometimes their curiosity will cause them to stray from the group. When they do, the consequences are often painful or deadly.

3. <u>Sheep are Fleers</u>: Sheep run from what frightens them. Animal behaviorists tell us that sheep have what is known as a flight zone similar to a human's comfort zone. You know what I am talking about. That invisible boundary line that we all have that when it is crossed, we feel violated and tend to move back. If a sheep's flight zone is compromised by what they perceive as a threat, they will run. They may not run far, but they will always run.

Okay. Let's review. 1. Natural born followers. 2. Social beings. 3. Tolerant of some in a group while suspicious of others. 4. Have an inherent need and desire for close personal relationships yet will abandon those relationships if threatened or if the grass appears to be greener on the other side of the fence. 5. When confronted with a threat, the first instinct is to run away from it. Move over Darwin and take your monkeys with you. Now I understand why one writer has characterized the nature of sheep as "the nature of sheeple." [8]

Let's change lanes from the history and generalities of sheep and shepherds and begin to focus on Psalm 23 from the perspective of the relationship between the sheep and the shepherd as the scripture frames it in a portrait of the relationship between God and his people. Let's begin with some general observations.

1. Psalm 23 is one of 74 Psalms that are identified as being written by David.

2. While the Bible provides an impressive resume of David's accomplishments, his formative years were spent caring for his father's sheep. He knew first-hand the relationship between the sheep and the shepherd.

3. Psalm 23 was probably written while David was in exile, hiding from Saul.

1 Samuel 18:10-11 tells of Saul becoming crazy with jealously toward David and trying to kill him. Verse 10: *"there was a spear in Saul's hand. And Saul cast the spear, for he said, "I will pin David to*

The Other Side of Psalm 23

the wall!" Verse 11 says *"But David eluded him."* (NKJV)

4. Psalm 23 is written from the perspective of the sheep.

5. Psalm 23:1 sets the stage for the other five verses: "The LORD is my shepherd, I shall not want." Let's unpack those nine words.

<u>*The*</u> in the context of Psalm 23:1 is used as a function word to indicate that a following noun is definite or has been previously specified by context or by circumstance. In other words, the noun that follows is something special, the real deal! It's not just the Lord, it's <u>*The*</u> Lord. The transcendent, omnipotent, omniscient, and omnipresent creative and sustaining force in the universe is my Lord!

The noun that follows is <u>*LORD*</u>. Notice anything unusual about how the word Lord is written? It is in all capital letters. Any time you see the word LORD in the Bible printed in all capital letters, it is identifying what is known as the Tetragrammaton. It is the four Hebrew letters YHWH, transliterated as *Yahweh*.

Yahweh is used wherever the Bible stresses God's personal relationship with his people and is printed LORD in all capital letters. It is used when the Bible wishes to present the personal character of God and his direct relationship with those human beings who have a special association with him. It is the personal name of God. G-o-d or the Hebrew Elohim, on the other hand, refers to God as the

Creator of the whole universe of people and things, and especially of the material world.

Look at Psalm 19. Notice verse one: "*The heavens are telling the Glory of God;*" That is the Hebrew Elohim that describes God's work in creation and his relationship to the material world.

Now move to verse seven: "*The law of the LORD is perfect...*" Here the psalmist switches to the topic of the law of the LORD and the relationship the LORD has with those who know him and follow his law. Lord is in capital letters. Elohim and LORD are both names of God the Father, that relate to different relationships with His creation.

So, when David says the <u>LORD</u>, he is affirming his close intimate relationship with the Father. The same kind of close relationship that exists between the sheep and the shepherd. That intimate relationship is affirmed with his use of the pronoun <u>*my*</u>.

<u>*Is*</u>, is a singular verb that means current and eternal. That's what I meant earlier when I said Psalm 23 is a psalm of life that encompasses the undeniable assurance of the provision and protection that God provides for the living. Because I have an intimate, current, and eternal relationship with the Father, <u>*I shall not want*</u>.

<u>*Shall*</u> in this context is the Hebrew khawsware and means absolute, no exception. *Shall* is a contemporary legal term that means an imperative command: no options; no choices; no mitigating

circumstances. Listen to how different translations, paraphrases, and literature word *I shall not want:*

I shall want nothing; How can I lack anything; I lack nothing; I shall lack for nothing; I shall not be in want; I have all I need; I will not be without any good thing; that's all I need; I will never be in need; I don't need a thing; Do you see it? Because I have an intimate, current, and eternal relationship with the Father, I shall lack for nothing.

What does it mean to lack for nothing? Look at Luke 12:27-31. I want you to notice something that I would imagine you have never noticed before. *"Consider the lilies, how they grow: they neither toil nor spin; yet I tell you, even Solomon in all his glory was not clothed like one of these. But if God so clothes the grass of the field, which is alive today and tomorrow is thrown into the oven, how much more will he clothe you—you of little faith!*

"And do not keep striving for what you are to eat and what you are to drink, and do not keep worrying. For it is the nations of the world that strive after all these things, and your Father knows that you need them. Instead, strive for his kingdom, and these things will be given to you as well." (NRSV)

Look at verse 32: *"Do not be afraid, little flock, for it is your Father's good pleasure to give you the kingdom."* Did you catch that? *"Do not be afraid, little flock..."* Flock, sheep, shepherd! With the Lord as my shepherd, not only will I lack for nothing, I won't have to worry about getting it.

I want you to notice one other thing from the Luke text. Jesus gives us two examples of *the things (that) will be given to you as well.* 1) Notice in verse 28 He uses the words *clothed, clothes,* and *clothe.* The New Testament Greek word for clothe is peribalo. It is a verb that means to protect. 2) In verse 29, he makes reference to "what you are to eat and drink."

Watch this! When the Lord is your shepherd, you will not lack for protection (clothes) or provision (food and drink); which are the very things that verses 2-6 of Psalm 23 assures us that the Lord our shepherd will provide for us.

The protection and provision of the shepherd for his sheep will be the topic for the next stop on our journey to the other side of Psalm 23.

Three

Green Pastures and Still Waters

The Geneva Bible, published in 1599, is one of the most historically significant translations of the Bible into English, preceding the King James translation by 51 years. This version of the Holy Bible is significant because, for the very first time, a mechanically printed, mass-produced Bible was made available directly to the general public. Also, for the first time, the Geneva Bible included brief study guides, collectively called apparatus, for each chapter.

> *"A Psalm of David. The Lord is my shepherd, I shall not want. He maketh me to rest in green pasture, and leadeth me by the still waters. He restoreth my soul, and leadeth me in the paths of righteousness for his*

> Name's sake. Yea, though I should walk through the valley of the shadow of death, I will fear no evil; for thou art with me: thy rod and thy staff, they comfort me. Thou dost prepare a table before me in the sight of mine adversaries: thou dost anoint mine head with oil, and my cup runneth over. Doubtless kindness and mercy shall follow me all the days of my life, and I shall remain a long season in the house of the Lord." (GBV)

"Consider the lilies, how they grow: they neither toil nor spin; yet I tell you, even Solomon in all his glory was not clothed like one of these. But if God so clothes the grass of the field, which is alive today and tomorrow is thrown into the oven, how much more will he clothe you—you of little faith!

"And do not keep striving for what you are to eat and what you are to drink, and do not keep worrying. For it is the nations of the world that strive after all these things, and your Father knows that you need them. Instead, strive for his kingdom, and these things will be given to you as well."

"Do not be afraid, little flock, for it is your Father's good pleasure to give you the kingdom." (NRSV)

Welcome to stop number three on our journey to discern the other side of Psalm 23. Let's begin by

The Other Side of Psalm 23

looking at how the shepherd provides protection and provision for his sheep. *The Lord is my shepherd, I shall not want...* (Psalm 23:2) *He makes me lie down in green pastures; he leads me beside still waters.* Before we explore these verses, I want to lay a couple of foundation blocks.

1. When the scripture says that the Shepherd makes the sheep lie down, *makes* in this context does not mean forcing the sheep to lie down. I'm not sure you can force sheep to do much of anything! Here the Old Testament word for *makes* is asah *(aw-saw')*. It's a verb that means to create favorable conditions; to provide opportunity; to ensure contentment.

2. In verse 2 and again in verse 3, the scripture uses the phrase, "he leads me..." When moving the flock from one location to another, the shepherd would never drive the sheep from behind; rather he would always walk in front of them or beside them so they could always have visual contact with him.

Because of their timid nature, it is almost impossible for sheep to lie down. In the course of my research for this series I have looked at over 300 photos of sheep. I have only been able to find two pictures of sheep lying down. Those two were of individual sheep lying down. I could not find any of an entire flock lying down.

Animal behaviorist tells us that because of their timid nature, it is impossible for sheep to lie down unless four requirements are met.

1. Sheep refuse to lie down unless they are free of all fear.
2. Being the social animal that they are, sheep will not lie down unless they are free from conflict with others in the group
3. Sheep refuse to lie down unless they are free from aggravations.
4. Sheep will not lie down as long as they are hungry or thirsty. Did you catch that?

For the sheep to be at rest they have to have to feel free from fear, tension, aggravations, hunger, and thirst. Works for me; How about you? Do you feel better when you're free from fear, free from tension, free from aggravations, and have your belly full? Move over Darwin and take your monkeys with you!

Freedom from fear, tension, aggravations, hunger, and thirst are all provided by the shepherd. As a matter of fact, the shepherd is the only one who can make it possible for them to lie down, to rest, to relax, to be content, quiet, and flourishing. Let's briefly look at how he does it.

1. Sheep refuse to lie down unless they are free of all fear. "Sheep are so timid and easily panicked that even a stray jackrabbit suddenly bounding from behind a bush can stampede a whole flock. Remember, sheep are followers. When one startled sheep runs in fright, a dozen others will bolt with it in blind fear."[9] Remember, sheep are fleers. *The*

Lord is my shepherd, I shall not want. He makes me lie down..."

Think about it! Think about the last time you were afraid; Think about the last time your fear triggered a panic attack; Think about the last time you were physically and mentally debilitated by the fear of the unknown; Think about how comforting and reassuring it was to know that you were not alone. *The Lord is my shepherd, I shall not want. He makes me lie down...* David put it this way in Psalm 46: *"God is our refuge and strength, an ever-present help in trouble. The LORD Almighty is with us;"*

An important part of my pastoral ministry over the years has been what I call the ministry of presence, especially in hospitals and medical emergencies. Hospitals and ER's are scary places, especially when we know something is wrong but we don't know what it is. The way I see it, the doctors, nurses, and technicians are there to determine the appropriate medical treatment. I am there to be a reminder that the *Lord is your shepherd*!

2. "Being the social animal that they are, sheep will not lie down unless they are free from friction with others in the group."[9] Conflict and jealousy within the flock will cause the sheep to become edgy, tense, discontented, and restless. They feel the need to *stand their ground*. Have you ever felt that way in a group? When the sheep see the shepherd, they tend to forget their rivalries and their need to

defend themselves from the group. In other words, when their focus is on the shepherd they are more likely to be at peace with one another.

Hmm! Does that sound familiar to anyone? In any human organization or group, especially a church, the one thing that can weaken and destroy their effectiveness is the loss of direction, mission, and purpose. And that happens when they lose their focus.

So, tell me. Any of you know what that loss of focus feels like? Have any of you ever witnessed how losing focus can derail the mission of an organization? Have any of you experienced how members of the group, including yourself, can get edgy, tense, discontented, and restless when they lose their focus? So, tell me. Any of you know how wonderful it feels to regain that focus? I do!

Do you see it? When our eyes are focused on our shepherd, all the stuff and junk of the world becomes secondary. When it becomes secondary, it takes less of our time and energy. It doesn't necessarily go away. Sometimes it's just not that big a deal anymore.

You suppose that's what the writer of Hebrews meant when he said: Hebrews 12:1-2: *"We have all these great people around us as examples. Their lives tell us what faith means. So we, too, should run the race that is before us and never quit. We should remove from our lives anything that would slow us down and the sin that so often makes us fall. We must never stop looking to Jesus. He is the leader of our faith, and he is the one who makes our faith complete."* (ERV)

3. Sheep refuse to lie down unless they are free from aggravations. Think for a minute about the last time you were aggravated about something. Now, while you are getting aggravated about the aggravation you are thinking about, let me give you some insight into aggravation.

The word aggravate comes from the Latin *aggravatus,* which means to make heavier, to make worse, to annoy or irritate. For me that definition implies that what aggravates me is usually not a big deal. If it was, I would simply get rid of it. I don't want to get rid of it, but sometimes it just really gets on my nerves, rubs me the wrong way, gets under my skin, puts me in a huff, a snit, and gets me steamed up, ticked off, and bent out of shape. Have I pretty well covered it for you?

Have you ever noticed how the more deliberate and intentional we are in keeping our eyes on Jesus, the more aggravations the devil throws at us to blur our focus and derail the good things that are happening?

I'm going to be honest and up-front with you today. I am aggravated! I am aggravated at my teenage dog! He's a little over two years old, and that in doggy years makes him a teenager. It's like he woke up one morning and decided he could do as he pleases, whenever he pleases.

Part of our going-to-bed routine is that the dog will go outside for a nite-nite pee-pee. He will then come in and we will all snuggle together for a restful night's sleep. A couple of nights ago, he decides he isn't ready to come in from his nite-nite pee-pee. He wants to stay out. I knew he wouldn't run off, so mamma and I went to bed. About an hour later, just as I am getting to the good part of my first dream, the dummy dog bangs on the door to come in.

So, I get up, open the door, and invite him in. What does he do? The moron just stands there looking at me. No matter what I say or what treat I offer him, he will not come in. After sharing my displeasure with his behavior, I shut the door and go back to what feels like a vibrating bed; vibrating because my wife is laughing so hard at me, which of course dumps aggravation on top of aggravation.

This routine goes on all night, every hour, until about 6:00 am. When he knocks on the door this time, I open it with fire in my eyes and his choke leash in my hand. If I have to go outside in my underwear and drag the stupid dog across the yard, so be it! When he sees the choke leash, what does he do? He calmly walks around me into the house and goes in the bedroom and lies down on my vibrating bed.

My teenage dog's behavior was not necessarily a big deal. I certainly wasn't going to get rid of him although the term dog pound did enter into one of my conversations with him. His rebellious behavior

The Other Side of Psalm 23

at the time simply put me in a huff, a snit, got me steamed up and ticked off.

While I am at it, something else that aggravates me is flies. You ever notice that when you are sitting outside on the deck or at a park, there is never a fly around. But the minute you put food out, you are bombarded by a swarm of the pesky annoying creatures and you wonder what God was thinking when he created them in the first place?

Believe it or not, the one thing that aggravates sheep the most are flies. In particular, the obligate parasite fly known as the nasal or bot fly. In the summer, they will buzz around the sheep's head, "attempting to deposit their eggs on the damp, mucous membranes of the sheep's nose."[9] It drives them crazy. They will start bleating or screaming, shaking their heads, and stomping their feet. Really? All that over just a *fly in the ointment*?

Once again, it is the shepherd who provides relief for the sheep. He doesn't necessarily get rid of the flies, he just helps the sheep to effectively deal with them. We will look at this aspect of the relationship of the sheep and shepherd in more detail when we get to verse five: *you anoint my head with oil...*

4. Finally, sheep will not lie down as long as they are hungry or thirsty. *He makes me to lie down in green pastures; he leads me beside still waters.*

It's ironic that most of the sheep producing countries in the world are dry, semi-arid areas, with green pastures and sources of clean water being few and far between. For example, Palestine, where David wrote this Psalm and kept his father's flocks, especially near Bethlehem, is a dry, brown, sun-burned wasteland. Consequently, it was the responsibility of the shepherd to ensure that there was ample pasture land for his sheep to eat and there was always a source of clean water for them to drink.

Have you ever wondered why David specifies *green* pastures and *still* waters? Remember, everything in the Bible is there for a purpose. Nothing in scripture is there by chance or coincidence. Every phrase and every word are there for a reason. So why "green" pastures and "still" waters? In ancient Palestine, there was more than one food source for sheep.

1. After a field of grain was harvested and the poor were able to gather their share, the shepherd would bring his sheep in to feed on what was left.

2. Parts of Judea were carpeted in the spring with a limited amount of grass that would quickly dry out in the summer heat. The resulting hay would be used as food for the sheep.

3. The most desirable food source for sheep were pastures of lush, green grass that the sheep could graze on throughout the day. My shepherd sources tell me that a typical flock would begin grazing as early as 3:30 in the morning. Apparently, the blades of grass were fuller early in the morning and the heavy dew would make them easier to chew.

4. I find it interesting that the color green in the Bible symbolizes healing, new beginnings, and restoration. You suppose that might have anything to do with verse three, *he restores my soul*?

"Although sheep thrive in dry, semi-arid country, they still require lots of water."[9] When sheep are thirsty, they become restless and begin to stray from the flock, looking for a drink. If a clean, purer water supply is not available, the sheep will end up drinking from polluted pot holes that are full of liver fluke parasites. Liver fluke disease has been known to wipe out whole herds of sheep.

Water for sheep came from three main sources:

1) The heavy dew on the early morning pasture grass.

2) Deep wells that are used when other sources are not readily available.

3) Springs, streams and pools of water.

When shepherds had to carry water to the flock from wells they would fill the bucket or trough to the brim. A full bucket was easier than a nearly empty bucket to drink from. What I find fascinating is that in mid-eastern culture a full cup is a sign of hospitality. To keep a guest's cup topped off conveyed the message, *you are welcome, safe, and secure here. Please feel free to stay as long as you like.* You suppose there might be a connection between full water troughs and verse five: *my cup overflows*?

Did you know that sheep will not drink from swiftly running water?

Two reasons:

1) Because of their timid nature, the noise will frighten them.

2) They are poor swimmers. If their wool coat becomes soaked with water the weight will pull the sheep under water. Instinctively sheep know this, so they will not go near swiftly running water.

Do you see how it all comes together? When the Psalmist tells us that the Lord is our shepherd and He makes us to lie down in green pastures and beside still waters, he is assuring us the Lord will always give us the best he has to offer.

The Lord is my shepherd, I shall not want (because he knows what I need, when I need it, and how I need it); Including green pastures, still waters, restoration of my soul, and spiritual direction, which is where we will begin Chapter 4.

Four

Help! I've fallen and I can't get up!

By the 1580's, the Roman Catholic Church saw that it had lost the battle to suppress the will of God: that His Holy Word would be available in the common English language. Thus, in 1582, the Church of Rome surrendered their fight for "Latin only" and decided that if the Bible was to be available in English, they would at least have an official Roman Catholic English translation.

Because it was translated at the Roman Catholic College in the city of Rheims, it was known as the Rheims New Testament. The Douay Old Testament was translated by the Church of Rome in 1609 at the College in the city of Douay. The combined product is commonly referred to as the "Douay/Rheims" Bible.

> *A psalm for David.* "*The Lord ruleth me: and I shall want nothing. He hath set me in a place of pasture. He hath brought me up, on the water of refreshment: he hath converted my soul. He hath led me on the paths of justice, for his own name's sake. For though I should walk in the midst of the shadow of death, I will fear no evils, for thou art with me. Thy rod and thy staff, they have comforted me. Thou hast prepared a table before me against them that afflict me. Thou hast anointed my head with oil; and my chalice which overflows me, how goodly is it! And thy mercy will follow me all the days of my life. And that I may dwell in the house of the Lord unto length of days.*" (DRA)

"Help! I've fallen and I can't get up!" Have you heard that one? It's the tagline for commercials advertising *Life Alert*, a Personal Emergency Response and Home Medical Alert company that was founded in 1987. It provides 24/7 electronic monitoring services for medical emergencies, fire protection, Carbon Monoxide gas leaks, and home intrusion. According to their website, *lifealert.com*,

The Other Side of Psalm 23

426,097 persons have been provided assistance by the system since 2008.

While the technology is much more sophisticated, the life alert process has been around for a long time. As a matter of fact, I found one that goes back thousands of years. Its tagline is, *The LORD is my shepherd, I shall not want.*

1. With the Lord as my shepherd, not only will I lack for nothing, I won't have to worry about getting it.

2. With the Lord as my shepherd, I will not lack for protection or provision. I will not lack provision for my physical needs because, *He makes me lie down in green pastures and He leads me beside still waters.* He provides for me from the fullness of his creation. An assurance of physical provision echoed by Jesus in John 10:10-11, when he says: *"I am the good shepherd. My purpose is to give life in all its fullness."* (TLB)

3. With the Lord as my shepherd, I will not lack for protection or provision. I will not lack provision for my emotional needs because, "He makes me lie down in green pastures and He leads me beside still waters." An assurance of emotional provision restated by David in Psalm 46: *"God is our refuge and strength, an ever-present help in trouble. The LORD Almighty is with us,"* providing for us freedom from fear, tension, and aggravations. An assurance of emotional provision echoed by Jesus

in John 14:1, when he says: *"Do not let your hearts be troubled. Trust in God; trust also in me."*

An assurance of emotional provision affirmed by the Apostle Peter in 1 Peter 5:7, when he says: *"Give all your worries and cares to God, for he cares about what happens to you."* (TLB)

The Lord is my shepherd, I shall not want. He makes me lie down in green pastures; he leads me beside still waters. Any questions? Okay. Now comes the hard part.

Psalm 23:3: *"He restores my soul. He leads me in paths of righteousness for his name's sake."* I find the thought of restoring my soul and leading me in the direction I need to go, reassuring and empowering. However, in the context of Psalm 23, it raises what I think is a legitimate question. If the psalm is written from the perspective of the sheep, then why the statement, "He restores my soul?" Doesn't it make sense that if the sheep are under the constant care of the shepherd, how could they ever become so distressed in soul that they would be in need of restoration? Two thoughts here:

1. David, the author of the Psalm, knew what it was like to be cast down, dejected, in need of soul restoration. He was well acquainted with the bitterness of feeling hopeless, helpless, and without strength in himself.

2. *"He restores my soul"* reflects a condition sheep often find themselves in that is called "cast" or "cast down." "Cast" or "cast down" sheep is a

common shepherd's term for a sheep that has turned over on its back and cannot get up again by itself. *Baahh! I've fallen and I can't get up!*

According to my shepherd consultant, "A "cast" sheep is a very pathetic site. Lying on its back, its feet in the air, it flays away frantically struggling to stand up, without success. Sometimes it will bleat a little for help, but generally it lies there lashing about in frightened frustration. If the shepherd does not arrive on the scene within a reasonably short time, the sheep will die." [9]

Here's how it happens. "A heavy, fat, or long fleeced sheep will lie down in some little hollow or depression in the ground. It may roll on its side slightly to stretch out or relax. If they roll over on their side far enough, their center of gravity will shift and cause them to roll on their back far enough that their feet no longer touch the ground. Feeling a sense of panic, they start to paw frantically, which only makes things worse.

"Their intense struggling causes gases to build up in their rumen or lower intestines. As the gases expand, the increased pressure will restrict or cut off blood circulation to their legs. If it is in the summer, a cast sheep can die in a few hours. If it is cool and cloudy and rainy it may survive in this position for several days."[9]

When a sheep goes missing from the flock, the first thing that usually comes to mind for the shepherd is that they are cast down somewhere.

Without hesitation, he will leave the flock and go search for the lost sheep. When he finds it, he immediately rolls it back on its feet. Sometimes, because of their weakened condition, the shepherd will have to carry the sheep back to the flock. And you know what? I'm glad he does!

From Luke 15:4-7: *"Which one of you, having a hundred sheep and losing one of them, does not leave the ninety-nine in the wilderness and go after the one that is lost until he finds it? When he has found it, he lays it on his shoulders and rejoices. And when he comes home, he calls together his friends and neighbors, saying to them, 'Rejoice with me, for I have found my sheep that was lost. Just so, I tell you, there will be more joy in heaven over one sinner who repents than over ninety-nine righteous persons who need no repentance."* (NRSV)

Without hesitation, the shepherd will leave the flock and go search for the lost sheep. I'm glad he does, because I often find myself spiritually cast down, helpless and afraid, immobilized with the fear that I may not recover. The one area of my life where I seem to trip, stumble, and fall the most is in my spiritual life; my connection to God; my focus on Jesus.

Don't for one-minute think that pastors are endowed with some sort of divine hazard avoidance system. I can hit those spiritual potholes with the best of them. Folks, there are times when I have fallen so hard, I have questioned whether or not I

The Other Side of Psalm 23

could get up, or if I even wanted to get up. It is in those moments that I have called on my divine life alert to restore my soul. "Help me dear Lord! I've fallen and I can't get up!"

One of the greatest revelations of the word of God is that Jesus, *"the Good shepherd"* (John 10:10), Jesus *"the Great shepherd"* (Hebrews 13:20), Jesus *"the Chief shepherd"* (1 Peter 5:4) has the same sense of anxiety, concern and compassion for cast people like you and me as the shepherd does for cast sheep. From Hebrews 2:18: *"Because he himself was tested by what he suffered, he is able to help those who are being tested."* (NRSV)

I want to direct your attention to three basic principles and parallels that I think will help us to grasp the way in which we can become "cast down."

1. Looking for a soft spot.
2. Too much wool.
3. Resistant to change.

I want to use the book of Revelation to frame these principles and parallels. First, a little context background.

1. The entire book of Revelation focuses on the conditions and events that will culminate with the promised return or second coming of Jesus into the world.

2. The first three chapters of Revelation are a series of messages directed at seven ancient churches that were in Asia Minor: Ephesus, Smyrna,

Pergamum, Thyatira, Sardis, Philadelphia, and Laodicea.

3. In the context of Revelation, these seven churches are used as examples of the churches and attitudes that will be found among Christian churches prior to the return of Jesus. I want to zero in on the church at Laodicea because I think it best reflects the principles and parallels between caste sheep and cast Christians.

1) <u>Looking for a soft spot</u>. The sheep that will most likely need rescue and restoration is the one who lets their desire for comfort get in the way of their need for connection with the shepherd. When they wander off from the flock, they lose sight of the shepherd and put themselves and the rest of the flock in jeopardy.

The folks at the Church of Laodicea were in danger of being cast because they were complacent, comfortable in their comfort zone. The Message paraphrase of Revelation 3:15-17 puts it this way: *"I know you inside and out and find little to my liking. You're not cold, you're not hot—far better to be either cold or hot! You're stale. You're stagnant. You make me want to vomit."* (MSG)

The Laodicea Christians ascribed to the theology of easy street. They let their desire for comfort get in the way of their need for connection with the shepherd. They were like a cartoon I saw years ago. The setting was the pastor's study. There was a couple sitting across the desk from the pastor. The caption read: *Pastor we are interested in joining the church. We were wondering if you might have some sort of non-participating option available?*

2) <u>Too much wool</u>. "Often when the fleece of a sheep becomes long, and matted down with mud, manure, burrs and other stuff, it is much easier for them to become cast, literally weighed down with its own wool."[9] Just as the Laodicea Christians enjoyed the comfort of their comfort zone, they also enjoyed their possessions. Back to the Message, verse 17: *"You brag, 'I'm rich, I've got it made, I need nothing from anyone,' oblivious that in fact you're a pitiful blind beggar, threadbare and homeless."* (MSG)

Don't get me wrong. There is nothing wrong with having stuff as long as you are in control of the stuff rather than the stuff being in control of you. The Laodicea Christians let their desire for stuff get in the way of their need for connection with the shepherd.

They either forgot or chose to ignore the parable of the rich fool that Jesus taught in Luke 12:12-21: *"Then someone called from the crowd, "Teacher, please tell my brother to divide our father's estate with me." Jesus replied, "Friend, who made me a judge over you to decide such things as that?"* (TLB)

Then he said, "Beware! Don't be greedy for what you don't have. Real life is not measured by how much we own." And he gave an illustration: *"A rich man had a fertile farm that produced fine crops. In fact, his barns were full to overflowing. So, he said, 'I know! I'll tear down my barns and build bigger ones. Then I'll have room enough to store everything. And I'll sit back and say to myself, my friend, you have enough stored away for years to come. Now take it easy! Eat, drink, and be merry!' "But God said to him, 'You fool! You will die this very night. Then who will get it all?' "Yes, a person is a fool to store up earthly wealth but not have a rich relationship with God."* (TLB)

The fat, long fleeced sheep that decided to replace his focus on the shepherd with his desire to find a soft comfortable spot would set himself up for a wake-up call that could be deadly. You think that's what Jesus meant when he said: 'You fool! You will die this very night. Then who will get it all?' You do know don't you that there are no self-storage units in heaven?

3) <u>Resistant to change</u>. Sheep are notorious creatures of habit. If left to themselves they will follow the same trails until they become ruts; graze the same hills until they turn to desert wastes; pollute their own ground until it is corrupt with disease and parasites. Because they are creatures of habit, if given the opportunity a sheep will return to the same comfort spots that got them in trouble in the first place. The more they roll and kick, the more the spot will be worn down.

The Other Side of Psalm 23

The more these spots are worn down, the more the possibility exists that they will become infested with potentially deadly parasites. If casting doesn't kill the sheep, infection will. Because of their flocking nature, when one sheep becomes infected, the whole flock is in jeopardy of being infected.

The one strategy that the shepherd has to protect his flock from becoming infected is to keep them on the move, leading the sheep to new pastures and new water supplies. Psalm 23:3: *"he restores my soul. He leads me in paths of righteousness for his name's sake."* A couple of footnotes here:

1. In the context of 23, the Old Testament Hebrew word for "soul" is nephesh (nephesh) and means life.

2. In the context of 23, the Old Testament Hebrew word for "righteousness" is ntsadaq (ntsadaq) and means moving toward restoration.

Do you see it? It is the task of the shepherd to protect the life of the sheep by constantly moving them in the direction of new opportunities for growth and restoration. And it is only when the sheep keep their eyes focused on the shepherd and follow his leading will they strive and flourish.

Folks I am convicted and convinced that for a church to experience real restoration, they have to be willing to risk change; to venture into new pastures; and keep their eyes on Jesus, our shepherd!

Alan Schmitt

"The Lord is my shepherd, I shall not want. He makes me lie down in green pastures; he leads me beside still waters; he restores my soul. He leads me in paths of righteousness for his name's sake."

Five

The Tools of the Trade

"The LORD is my shepherd; I shall not want. He maketh me to lie down in green pastures: he leadeth me beside the still waters. He restoreth my soul: he leadeth me in the paths of righteousness for his name's sake. Yea, though I walk through the valley of the shadow of death, I will fear no evil: for thou art with me; thy rod and thy staff they comfort me. Thou preparest a table before me in the presence of mine enemies: thou anointest my head with oil; my cup runneth over. Surely goodness and mercy shall follow me all the days of my life: and I will dwell in the house of the LORD forever." (KJV)

Welcome to stop number five on our journey to the Other Side of Psalm 23.

In this and Chapter 6, our focus is going to be on verse four and the first line of verse five. "*Yea, though I walk through the valley of the shadow of death, I will fear no evil; for you are with me; your rod and your staff, they comfort me. You prepare a table before me in the presence of my enemies;* (KJV)

In order to put this passage in perspective, I'm going to mix things up a little bit. Allow me to explain why.

1. I want us to first look at the tools of the trade for shepherds and how they were used to provide provision and protection for the sheep. I believe when we do, we will gain a better understanding of the divine tools our shepherd uses to provide provision and protection for us.

2. Preparing a table for the sheep, in the presence of their enemies, was what required them to walk through the valley of the shadow of death. So, we're going to mix things up a little bit. You with me?

1. <u>The tools of the trade</u>: The shepherds garb, his grub, and his gear.

1) The common garb of the shepherd was a simple tunic of cotton that was girded around his body by a wide leather belt or girdle. He would also carry with him an outer garment called an abaya (abaya) that was typically made of camel's hair. The

The Other Side of Psalm 23

abaya would serve as a rain coat, an over coat, and a blanket at night.

Tradition tells us that when John the Baptist father, Zacharias, was not performing his monthly duties as a priest at the temple in Jerusalem, he and his family had a small sheep farm. Since John was the only son, he was assigned the responsibility of shepherd for his father's flock. Apparently, when he left the family farm to begin his preaching ministry, he continued to wear the traditional garb of a shepherd. Matthew 3:4: *"John's clothes were made of camel's hair, and he had a leather belt around his waist."*

2) Although Matthew tells us that John's diet consisted of locusts and wild honey, the more common <u>grub</u> of the shepherd was an assortment of fruits and vegetables including olives, onions, garlic, leeks, lentils, beans, cucumbers, melons, grapes, pomegranates, figs, dates, and almonds, what we today would call a health conscience diet.

3) The <u>gear</u> of the shepherd included:

1. <u>His shepherd's scrip</u>, which was a bag made of dried sheep skin; an early version of a backpack. He would use it to carry his food, ointment for the sheep, and rocks for his sling. You remember the story of a younger David and the Philistine giant Goliath: 1 Samuel 17:40: *"And he took his staff, which he had always in his hands: and chose him five smooth stones out of the brook, and put them into the shepherd's <u>scrip</u>, which he had with him,*

and he took a sling in his hand, and went forth against the Philistine." (DRA)

2. <u>His shepherd's sling.</u> It was a simple contraption. It consisted of two strings of sinew, rope, or leather with a leather pouch tied in the middle. To operate it, the shepherd would put a smooth stone in the pouch, sling it around his head a couple of times and let go of one of the strings.

In addition to using his sling against wild animals, robbers, and giants, the shepherds sling was also useful in keeping the sheep in line. A stone could be dropped behind a sheep that was lagging behind and startle it into coming along with the rest of the flock. Or if one would start to stray from the flock, then a stone would be slung so as to drop just beyond the straying sheep, and thus bring it back in line.

3. <u>The shepherd's flute</u>. The shepherds of ancient Palestine knew what modern day medical research has affirmed: Music can soothe the savage beast, including bored, lonely, and depressed shepherds; and timid, frightened, and tired sheep. The instrument of choice for the shepherd was the Chaliyl, a pipe that was perforated with holes, similar to a modern-day recorder, that was typically made from reeds, bone, or horns.

One writer put it this way: "When the music comes from the flute, the heart of the shepherd is stirred and the sheep of the flock are refreshed by the invigorating music that comes from this simple instrument. There can be little question but that David used such an instrument when he was with his flock, in the same way the shepherd lads have done for centuries around Bethlehem."[10]

I find it interesting to note that the word in the Arabic language that is the equivalent of the Hebrew word for "psalm" is mizmor (mizmor), which means "played on a pipe or flute." The two most important pieces of the shepherd's gear were his rod and his staff.

4. <u>The shepherd's rod</u> was traditionally made from a sapling of the Kermes or Palestine oak, a type of evergreen oak tree indigenous to ancient Palestine. The rod would range in length from two to four feet long, depending on the size and preference of the shepherd. The root of the sapling would be carved and whittled down to form a round knob. Although simple in design, the shepherd's rod served a number of practical purposes.

1) It was used as an instrument of protection for both the shepherd and his sheep. It was his primary means of defense against anything that would threaten him or his flock. He would also use it to beat the brush discouraging snakes and other creepy-crawly creatures from disturbing the flock. The shepherd would also use his rod to drive off predators like coyotes, wolves, cougars, lions, and bears.

It was his experience in killing lions and bears that David used to convince Saul to let him take on

Goliath. 1 Samuel 17:34-37: *"I have been taking care of my father's sheep," he said. "When a lion or a bear comes to steal a lamb from the flock, I go after it with a club and take the lamb from its mouth. If the animal turns on me, I catch it by the jaw and club it to death. I have done this to both lions and bears, and I'll do it to this pagan Philistine, too, for he has defied the armies of the living God! The LORD who saved me from the claws of the lion and the bear will save me from this Philistine!"* (NTL)

2) A second use of the rod was to examine and count the sheep. In the terminology of the Old Testament this was referred to as passing "under the rod" A sheep that passed "under the rod" was one which had been counted and looked over to make sure they were okay.

In the evening, as the sheep were coming into the sheepfold, the shepherd would stop each one, open their fleece with his rod, and carefully run his hands over their body to examine the condition of the skin, the cleanliness of the fleece, and any signs of infection.

3) When a festival or holy day required a tithe offering, the shepherd would use the passing "under the rod" to determine which sheep would be chosen. Leviticus 27:32: *"The entire tithe of the herd and flock, every tenth animal that passes under the shepherd's rod, will be holy to the LORD."*

4) The primary use of the shepherd's rod, perhaps

more than any other, was for the discipline of the flock. If the shepherd saw a sheep that was straying from the flock into harm's way, "his rod would go whistling through the air to send the wayward soul scurrying back to the flock."[9]

An interesting footnote to the shepherd's rod is that it was seen as an extension of his own right arm. In doing so, it symbolized his strength, his power, and his authority to shepherd the flock.

The origin of the rod, as symbolizing the authority of the shepherd, finds it origins in the conversation between God and Moses, when God is calling Moses to lead the Israelites out of Egyptian slavery. Exodus 4:1-5: *"Then Moses answered and said, "But suppose they will not believe me or listen to my voice; suppose they say, 'The LORD has not appeared to you.'" So, the LORD said to him, "What is that in your hand?" He said, "A rod." And He said, "Cast it on the ground." So, he cast it on the ground, and it became a serpent; and Moses fled from it. Then the LORD said to Moses, "Reach out your hand and take it by the tail" (and he reached out his hand and caught it, and it became a rod in his hand), "that they may believe that the LORD God of their fathers, the God of Abraham, the God of Isaac, and the God of Jacob, has appeared to you."* (NKJV)

In verses 20 we are told that: *"Moses took his wife and his sons and set them on a donkey, and* *he returned to the land of Egypt. And Moses took the <u>rod of God in his hand</u>."*

5. <u>The shepherd's staff.</u> The shepherd's staff was the shepherd's badge. It identified the shepherd as a shepherd. No one in any other profession carried a shepherd's staff. It was a tool used exclusively for the care and management of sheep, and only sheep. Its design and shape were uniquely adapted to the needs of sheep.

You know what they looked like: They were a long slender stick, most likely made of Hazel wood that would vary in length depending on the size of the shepherd. As a general rule, they were as long as the shepherd was tall. The defining component of the staff was the hook on one end. It was used for a variety of sheep management purposes. I want to briefly list three.

1) During lambing season, the shepherd would use his staff to gently lift a newborn lamb and bring it to its mother if they become parted. In a large flock there were often dozens of lambs being born at the same time. It was easy for the ewe to lose her lamb in all of the confusion. The staff kept the shepherd from touching the lamb. If he did, his scent would cause the ewe to reject her newborn.

2) The shepherd's staff was used for guiding the sheep. While their instinct for flocking was strong, sometimes their curiosity would cause them to stray from the group. You know, that "grass is greener on the other side" thing. Sheep had a natural inclination

The Other Side of Psalm 23

to wander off. If one of them started to wander the shepherd would gently tap, nudge, or jab the end of his staff against the sheep's side and redirect them in the way he wanted them to go.

A subtle, yet effective part of the staff was a spoon-shaped "shovel" carved into the end. If the sheep started to wander, and the shepherd was not close enough to tap, nudge, or jab them back in line, he could scoop up a bit of mud or dirt and flick it at the sheep to catch their attention.

3) Another common use of the shepherd's staff was to rescue the sheep from all the precarious predicaments they would get themselves into. Like climbing down a steep cliff to get a morsel of grass and then forgetting how to climb back up; or getting to close to the edge of a stream or pond and falling in; or freeing them from a labyrinth of wild thorny brambles where they had pushed in to find a few stray mouthfuls of green grass.

Okay. The shepherds garb, his grub, and his gear. Any questions? Is anyone wanting to ask: What does our browsing through the shepherds' outfitter catalog have to do with the Lord is my shepherd? If so, you're in luck. I have an answer.

1. In the <u>context</u> of 23, the phrase "Thy rod and Thy staff," embodies all the tools that the shepherd had at his disposal to provide provision and protection for his sheep. In the <u>application</u> of 23, I believe the phrase "Thy rod and Thy staff," embodies all the tools that our shepherd uses to

provide provision and protection for you and me. There are four things I want to suggest are in the tool box of our shepherd:

1) <u>Grace:</u> I'm not sure that there any better an example of the grace of God than that reflected in the relationship between the shepherd and his sheep. It is a relationship rooted in the unconditional love of the shepherd for his sheep. Think about it. What else can you call living with a bunch of dumb, dependent, and defenseless followers, flockers, and fleer sheep, alone, 24/7, for months at a time, in the Judean wilderness!

You suppose God ever looks at us, shakes his head, and says you are such a bunch of dumb, dependent, and defenseless followers, flockers, and fleers! The writer of Isaiah seemed to think so. Isaiah 53:6: *"All of us have strayed away like sheep. We have left God's paths to follow our own."* I know he shakes his head at me, but that's okay, because I know that no matter how dumb, dependent, and defenseless I may ever be, he will still be my shepherd. A shepherd who would not hesitate to lay down his life for me. John 10:11: *"I am the good shepherd. The good shepherd lays down his life for the sheep."*

2) <u>A comprehensive owner's manual:</u> We recently purchased a new car that came with a comprehensive 652-page owner's manual. It includes a detailed description of what the car is, what the car is capable of doing, and how I am supposed to operate

it. When we accept the Lord as our shepherd, we are given a comprehensive divine owner's manual that contains the revealed, inspired, and illuminated record of who my shepherd is, who my shepherd wants to be, and who my shepherd wants me to be. It's called the Bible.

3) <u>Other sheep.</u> I am given the assurance that I am not alone. I know that I am part of a larger flock that are all headed down the same paths of righteousness. I am given the assurance that I will never have to walk alone through the valley of the shadow of fear, tension, aggravations, hunger, thirst, even death!

4) Without question, the most valuable tool in our shepherd's tool box is our divine GPS. God's Personal Shepherd. Ten days after Jesus our good, great, and chief shepherd ascended into heaven, God replaced him with a personal shepherd assigned to provide one-on-one provision and protection for each of us. Watch this!

John 14, beginning with verse 16: *"And I will pray the Father, and he shall give you another <u>Comforter</u> that he may abide with you forever..."* (NKJV) According to the dictionary, a comforter is someone who comforts you. Do you see it? The Lord is my shepherd, I shall not want. Thy rod and Thy staff, they <u>comfort</u> me!

2 Corinthians 1:3-6: *"Praise be to the God and Father of our Lord Jesus Christ, the Father of compassion and the God of all comfort, who*

Alan Schmitt

comforts us in all our troubles, for just as the sufferings of Christ flow over into our lives, so also through Christ our comfort overflows." The Lord is my shepherd, I shall not want. Thy rod and Thy staff, they comfort me!

Six

Tables and Valleys

A Psalm of David. *"The LORD is my shepherd; I shall not want. He makes me to lie down in green pastures; He leads me beside the still waters. He restores my soul; He leads me in the paths of righteousness For His name's sake. Yea, though I walk through the valley of the shadow of death, I will fear no evil; for You are with me; Your rod and Your staff, they comfort me. You prepare a table before me in the presence of my enemies; You anoint my head with oil; My cup runs over. Surely goodness and mercy shall follow me all the days of my life; And I will dwell in the house of the LORD Forever."* (NKJV)

Alan Schmitt

In June, 1996, I was inducted into the charter class of the Hillcrest High School Alumni Hall of Fame. Former Attorney General John Ashcroft and I shared a place at the head table that day. I remember sitting at the head table, looking out at many of my classmates who were not at the head table. Classmates, who had belittled, bullied, and branded as worthless, that skinny red-headed kid of thirty years prior.

I remember sitting at the head table, looking at all of them not sitting at the head table, and having two irresistible urges:

1. One was to begin my acceptance speech by quoting scripture; in particular Matthew 19:30: *"many who are first will be last, and many who are last will be first."*

2. The other urge I had was to proclaim with a loud and confident voice: *Nah, Nah, Nah, Nah, Nah!* For you see on that day in June, 1996, I was sitting at a table that had been prepared for me in the presence of my enemies. At least that's one scene I used to imagine when I would read verse four of Psalm 23. *"Thou preparest a table before me in the presence of mine enemies."*

Another picture that my mind's eye has painted over the years, on the bereavement side of 23, has been the *Welcome New Members* banquet that I get to attend on my arrival at the pearly gates. I reasoned that the "mine enemies" thing might be all those folks who were aggravated that I made it

The Other Side of Psalm 23

to heaven and they were forced to sit at the table with me.

As I began to look at 23 from the other side, especially framed in the shepherd providing provision and protection for his sheep, the word "table" began to take on a new and curious perspective. So, I did a little research and here's what I have come up with.

It was the responsibility of the shepherd to ensure that there was ample pasture land for his sheep to eat and there was always a source of clean water for them to drink.

In ancient Palestine, there was more than one food source for sheep.

1. After a field of grain was harvested and the poor were able to gather their share, the shepherd would bring his sheep in to feed on what was left.

2. Parts of Judea were carpeted in the spring with a limited amount of grass that would quickly dry out in the summer heat. The resulting hay would be used as food for the sheep.

3. The most desirable food source for sheep were pastures of lush, green grass, that the sheep could graze on throughout the day. The most desirable pastures of lush, green grass, were typically found in the high mountain country. These high mountain flat-topped plateaus of lush, green grass were called alplands, table lands, or mesas, the Spanish word for table.

In the spring, before all the snow was melted, the shepherd would take scouting trips into the high mountain country to stake his claim on the lushest and greenest pasture land he could find. A few weeks before it was time to move the sheep, the shepherd would once again travel into the high mountain country. During this trip, he would make final preparations for the arrival of his sheep.

1. He would remove any poisonous weeds and briers that could endanger or entangle the sheep.

2. He would clear out the water holes, springs and drinking places that had become overgrown with grass, brush, and weeds

3. If necessary, the shepherd would build small earth dams to channel the spring water into pools of still waters.

4. Before returning to the sheep, the shepherd would also look for any spoor of potential predator enemies of the sheep, such as coyotes, bears, wolves or cougars. The term "spoor" means tracks, scents, scat, or broken foliage that would indicate the presence of the natural enemies of the sheep. If he knew which predators were in the area, the shepherd could better equip himself to defend his sheep in the event of an attack.

I didn't know until recently that a phrase common in politics is *look carefully at the spoor on the trails*. It means to carefully investigate what is actually going on in a particular situation

A favorite hiding spot for the sheep predators were the rim rocks that would surround the mountain tables. From these high hidden perches, the enemy could watch every movement of the sheep waiting for the opportune time to attack. Are you beginning to see the picture? *"Thou preparest a table before me in the presence of mine enemies."*

When it was time for the shepherd to move his flock to the high mountain tablelands, the route of choice was through the gulches, ravines and valleys that would wind their way through the mountains.

The shepherd knew that the valleys would provide a gentle grade for the sheep to climb, along with an abundance of forage for them to eat along the way. He also knew that the melting snow from the higher elevations would create gently flowing streams of water for the sheep to drink.

While the valleys were the route of choice, they also posed an assortment of deadly dangers along the way.

1. Because of the towering cliffs above them on each side, the valley floor was often dark, with the sun seldom reaching the bottom except for a few hours around high noon.

2. Rock slides, mud or snow avalanches, and flash floods were a constant threat.

3. The cliffs and rocky outcroppings provided perches for those pesky coyotes, bears, wolves, and cougars to watch every movement of the sheep, waiting for the opportune time to attack. There were more sheep killed in the valleys than anywhere else because when a predator would attack, the escape routes available to the sheep were limited.

You beginning to see this picture? *"Yea, though I walk through the valley of the shadow of death, I will fear no evil:"* Interesting, isn't it, how it now begins to come together and make sense.

I want you to notice something that is often overlooked in reading 23; an overlooked subtlety that I believe has a profound message.

1. Notice in verses 2-3, David refers to God in the third person:

<u>He</u> makes me to lie down in green pastures; <u>He</u> leads me beside the still waters. <u>He</u> restores my soul; <u>He</u> leads me in the paths of righteousness

For <u>His</u> name's sake.

2. In verses 4-5, David begins referring to God in the second person:

Yea, though <u>I</u> walk through the valley of the shadow of death, <u>I</u> will fear no evil; For <u>You</u> are with me; <u>Your</u> rod and <u>Your</u> staff, they comfort me.

<u>You</u> prepare a table before me in the presence of my enemies;

<u>You</u> anoint my head with oil; <u>My</u> cup runs over.

3. Then in verse 6, he returns to the third person:

Surely goodness and mercy shall follow me all the days of my life; And I will dwell in the house of the LORD forever.

Do you see it? In verses 2-3 David is talking <u>about</u> the Lord, his shepherd.

In verses 4-5, David is talking <u>to</u> the Lord, his shepherd. It's subtle but it's there. The obvious question is why? Here's my take on it.

The Other Side of Psalm 23

When life is good; when we are experiencing the green grass, still waters, provision of God in our life; when our soul is feeling restored and we feel like our life is headed in the right direction, we may occasionally offer up an obligatory prayer of thanksgiving. We know he is there; we know that our lack of want is because of him; Yea, we know that he is our shepherd.

When life sucks; when we feel overwhelmed by the vastness of the physical or emotional ravines we find ourselves in; when we find ourselves walking through the valley of the shadow fear, discouragement, abandonment, uncertainty, those crisis moments in our life, that's when we need him to be there, to pull out the rod of restoration and the staff of salvation; to comfort us in the presence of all our real or contrived enemies.

One writer put it this way: "We're more prone to talk about God when we are in the green pastures and more prone to talk to God when we're in the dangerous ravine. In the light, we are prone to wander off in pursuit of greener grass. But in the dark, we hug His knee." [11]

The LORD is your shepherd, in good times and bad! In green pastures and in dark valleys!

I want you to notice one additional subtlety. Look again at verse 4: "Yea, though I walk through the valley…" You see it? I walk <u>through</u> the valley, not I am stuck in the valley; not I am lost in the

Alan Schmitt

valley; not I am consumed by the valley; not I will never make it out of the valley alive.

No matter how deep, dark, and dreadful our personal valley may ever be, with the Lord as our shepherd, we will always make it through.

Seven

What is a Shepherd Church?

Psalm 23:1-6 – 1 Peter 5:1-4 – John 10:1-18

Three of my favorite TV shows are *Blue Bloods*, *Chicago PD*, and *NCIS New Orleans*. While the storylines, locations, and characters are all different, one thing that they all have in common are their badges. Whether it be Detective Danny Reagan, Captain Hank Voight, or Special Agent Dwayne Pride, somewhere in the course of the show they will all flash their badges to identifying who they are.

Think about this. What if as Christians we used a badge to identify who we are? What if instead of Detective, Captain, or Special Agent, it was inscribed with the title Shepherd. What if instead of the insignia on the badge being the seal of the City of New York, the city of Chicago, or the City of New Orleans, it was a picture of a shepherd with his sheep? What would it represent? When someone saw it, really saw it, for the first time, what would it mean?

Consider this. When I think of what a police officer's badge represents, three things come to mind:

1) The personal integrity of the officer.
2) Under what authority do they act?
3) What is the range and scope of the services they provide?

I would like to apply those three reflections to the badge of a shepherd church.

1. <u>Personal integrity of its members</u>. A couple of thoughts here.

1) The integrity of a member of a shepherd church is rooted in their accepting Jesus Christ as their Savior, their Lord, and their Shepherd. Their words and actions echo the words of David when he declares, "The LORD is my Shepherd. Say it with me: "The Lord is my Shepherd." Say it again: "The LORD is my Shepherd."

Now, I'm not going to ask if you really know what that means because hopefully, after reading this book, you have gained a working understanding of what "The LORD is my shepherd" truly means.

2) The integrity of a member of a shepherd church is witnessed in their deliberate and intentional affirmation, by their words and actions, that because the Lord is their shepherd, they lack for nothing. They repeat the words of David when he confidently asserts, "The LORD is my Shepherd.

I shall not want." Say that with me: "I shall not want." Say it again: "I shall not want." Are you sure? Are you really sure?

Remember, sheep are dumb, dependent, defenseless, followers, flockers, and fleers, who are totally at the mercy of – cannot survive without – a constant connection with their shepherd. Do you have a constant connection with your shepherd?

You know it's easy to declare, "The Lord is my shepherd. I shall not want," on a Sunday morning, snug in the safety and security of the church sheep pen, while surrounded by other like-minded sheep.

What about when you walk out the door of this sheep pen and venture back into the valleys of the daily routine of your lives. Is he still your shepherd then? Do you rely on his provision and protection for everything in your life, every day of your life?

I once had a church member challenge me when I would share what I call God moments. His observation was, "Did you ever think that what you call God moments might in reality just be random coincidences that you are reading something into?" My answer was absolutely! What I read into them is an acknowledgment that the Lord, my shepherd, is the source of the provision and protection for everything in my life!

It should come as no surprise to anyone that we are living in a world today in which the integrity of the church is being called into question. The honesty, sincerity, and consistency of the divine truths we represent are being scrutinize under the highest power lens of the microscope of integrity.

If we only had extreme examples of integrity meltdown to deal with, we could probably survive. What concerns me is that the lab report for many regular churches is revealing a diagnosis of severe integrity anemia. How do we keep that from happening in a Shepherd Church?

1. We must never forget that the integrity of the church is only as strong as the integrity of its members.

2. We must never forget that the strength, wellness, and integrity of the members of a Shepherd Church is only as strong as the affirmation of their words and actions that the Lord is their Shepherd.

2) <u>Under what authority do the members of a Shepherd Church act?</u>

As an introduction to the question of authority, I want to draw your attention John 10:1-18: *"Very truly I tell you Pharisees, anyone who does not enter the sheep pen by the gate, but climbs in by some other way, is a thief and a robber. The one who enters by the gate is the shepherd of the sheep. The gatekeeper opens the gate for him, and the sheep listen to his voice. He calls his own sheep by name and leads them out.*

"When he has brought out all his own, he goes on ahead of them, and his sheep follow him because they know his voice. But they will never follow a stranger; in fact, they will run away from him

because they do not recognize a stranger's voice." Jesus used this figure of speech, but the Pharisees did not understand what he was telling them.

"Therefore, Jesus said again, "Very truly I tell you, I am the gate for the sheep. All who have come before me are thieves and robbers, but the sheep have not listened to them. I am the gate; whoever enters through me will be saved. They will come in and go out and find pasture. The thief comes only to steal and kill and destroy; I have come that they may have life and have it to the full.

"I am the good shepherd. The good shepherd lays down his life for the sheep. The hired hand is not the shepherd and does not own the sheep. So, when he sees the wolf coming, he abandons the sheep and runs away. Then the wolf attacks the flock and scatters it. The man runs away because he is a hired hand and cares nothing for the sheep.

"I am the good shepherd; I know my sheep and my sheep know me— just as the Father knows me and I know the Father—and I lay down my life for the sheep. I have other sheep that are not of this sheep pen. I must bring them also. They too will listen to my voice, and there shall be one flock and one shepherd. The reason my Father loves me is that I lay down my life—only to take it up again. No one takes it from me, but I lay it down of my own accord. I have authority to lay it down and authority to take it up again. This command I received from my Father."

Alan Schmitt

The words of Jesus recorded by John speak a profound acknowledgment of the unconditional love of God that was revealed in the person of Jesus, the good shepherd:

Verse 11: "*I am the good shepherd. The good shepherd lays down his life for the sheep.*"

Verse 14-15: "*I am the good shepherd. I know my own and my own know me, just as the Father knows me and I know the Father. And I lay down my life for the sheep.*"

Verse 18: "*No one takes it from me, but I lay it down of my own accord. I have power to lay it down, and I have power to take it up again. I have received this command from my Father.*"

I want you to notice something that is often overlooked in reading this familiar passage. Sandwiched between those profound acknowledgments of the unconditional love of God is an equally profound challenge to be a shepherd church. Look at verse 16: "*I have other sheep that do not belong to this fold. I must bring them also, and they will listen to my voice. So there will be one flock, one shepherd.*"

Listen to how the Contemporary English Version words it: "*I have other sheep that are not in this sheep pen. I must bring them together too, (so that) when they hear my voice… there will be (one flock and one shepherd).*" (CEV)

The word "voice" is the key here. Under what

authority do the members of a Shepherd Church act? The voice of God.

In verses 3-4 of our text from John, Jesus makes reference to the voice of the shepherd on two different perspectives: Verse 3: "the sheep recognize his voice." Verse 4: the sheep "are familiar with his voice."

It is the voice of the shepherd that the sheep will follow because they recognize it and they trust it. I believe that the witness of scripture affirms that the church has been given a divine mandate to be the shepherd voice of God.

Matthew 28:18-20: *"All authority in heaven and on earth has been given to me. Therefore, go and make disciples of all nations ... teaching them..."*

Matthew 10:19-20: *"And do not worry about what to say or how to say it. At that time, you will be given what to say, for it will not be you speaking, but the Spirit of your Father speaking through you."*

Acts 20:28-32: (This is Paul speaking to the church at Ephesus just before he leaves to go to Jerusalem) *"Keep watch over yourselves and over all the flock, of which the Holy Spirit has made you overseers, to shepherd the church of God that he obtained with the blood of his own Son. I commend you to God and to the message of his grace, a message that is able to build you up and to give you the inheritance among all who are sanctified. Now I'm turning you over to God, our marvelous God who's gracious Word can make you into what he wants you to be and give you everything you could possibly need in this community of holy friends."*

At your church do you speak the voice of God? I hope you are. We all better be speaking the voice of God, because if we don't, the voice of God will be drowned out by the voices of evil. Voices of evil who are committed to hijacking the Gospel, looting the message of grace and mercy, and, as our text from John warns, sneaking into the sheep pen with the intent to steal, kill, and destroy.

3. <u>A shepherd church is a faith community who cares for people in a way that shows.</u> Acts 20:28: *"Keep watch over yourselves and over all the flock, of which the Holy Spirit has made you overseers, to shepherd the church of God that he obtained with the blood of his own Son."*

From 1 Peter 5:1-4: "Just as shepherds watch over their sheep, you must watch over everyone God has placed in your care... set an example for them." (CEV)

From 2 Corinthians 1:3-7: *"All praise to the God and Father of our Master, Jesus the Messiah! Father of all mercy! God of all healing counsel! He comes alongside us when we go through hard times, and before you know it, he brings us alongside someone else who is going through hard times so that we can be there for that person just as God was there for us."* (MSG)

From a paraphrase of Psalm 23: It is because of the shepherd church that I can lie down in green pastures when I need to lie down; It is because of the shepherd church that when I am thirsty I am led beside still waters;

It is the shepherd church that speaks to me the voice of God, words that I need to hear and actions I need to see to restore my soul.

It is the shepherd church that leads me in right paths when I am traveling down the wrong path. When I find myself walking through the darkest valley, my shepherd church is there, with me, protecting me, comforting me, feeding me, and anointing me.

If you haven't picked up on it yet, there a lot of folks in your community who are caste down, not having the strength to get up on their own. There are folks who come in the doors of your church on a regular basis who are entangled in the thorns and briers of addiction, family dysfunctions, financial desperation, and strained relationships.

The sheep of your pasture are constantly plagued by health aggravations and chronic disease. There are people sitting in churches ever Sunday who feel trapped in valleys of fear, discouragement, and frustration, overwhelmed by the height and darkness of the ravines closing in around them, living in the shadow of those selfish, uncaring predators who are waiting for the right moment to kill, steal and destroy. It seems to me that scripture, tradition, and experience all affirm that a shepherd church is a church who cares for those folks in a way that shows.

Alan Schmitt

Can we save the world? No! Just as the combined efforts of Detective Danny Reagan, Captain Hank Voight, and Special Agent Dwayne Pride cannot eradicate crime in the world, neither can we save all the sheep of the world.

If we cannot save all the sheep of the world, should we try to save any of the sheep of the world? Absolutely! Even if we are only able to save just one, that should be cause for celebration.

Jesus put it this way in Luke 15:4-7: *"Suppose one of you has a hundred sheep and loses one of them. Does he not leave the ninety-nine in the open country and go after the lost sheep until he finds it? And when he finds it, he joyfully puts it on his shoulders and goes home. Then he calls his friends and neighbors together and says, 'Rejoice with me; I have found my lost sheep.' I tell you that in the same way there will be more rejoicing in heaven over one sinner who repents than over ninety-nine righteous persons who do not need to repent."*

What makes a church a shepherd church?

1. The personal integrity of its members is rooted in their accepting Jesus Christ as their Savior, their Lord, and their Shepherd.

2. It speaks with authority the voice of God.

3. It cares for people in a way that shows.

How do you think your Church measures up? How do you think you measure up as a member of a shepherd church?

Epilogue

"The Lord is my shepherd; I shall not want. He maketh me to lie down in green pastures: he leadeth me beside the still waters. He restoreth my soul: he leadeth me in the paths of righteousness for his name's sake. Yea, though I walk through the valley of the shadow of death, I will fear no evil: for thou art with me; thy rod and thy staff they comfort me. Thou preparest a table before me in the presence of mine enemies: thou anointest my head with oil; my cup runneth over. Surely goodness and mercy shall follow me all the days of my life: and I will dwell in the house of the Lord forever." (KJV) Any questions?

I feel confident in saying that Psalm 23 will continue to be the most recognized bereavement passage of scripture in the Bible to both believers and non-believers alike. It has proven over and over again it's time-tested ability to soften the sting of death and provide comforting words of hope and assurance.

The bereavement side of Psalm 23 is important and necessary. It is my hope and prayer that having journeyed with me through the inspired words of David, you will now recognize that there is another side of Psalm 23!

References

1. Hawkins, Karla. *7 Of the Most Famous Bible Scriptures, The Christian Crier*, May 28, 2015. Retrieved from patheos.com/blogs/christiancrier/2015/05/28/7-of-the-most-famous-bible-scriptures/
2. Miles, C. Austin, "In The Garden," William Heinemann Ltd. Publishing, Covenant Garden, England, 1912. Public Domain.
3. Adams, Sarah Fowler, "Nearer My God to Thee." Lee & Shepard Publishing, Boston, MA, 1841. Public Domain.
4. Brock, Virgil P, "Beyond the Sunset." Word Music, LLC, Nashville, TN, 1936.
5. Anderson, Bernhard W., *Out of the Depths: The Psalms Speak for Us Today*, Philadelphia: The Westminster Press, 197, p. 144.
6. Challies, Tim, *Do More Better: A Practical Guide to Productivity*, Hudson, Ohio: Cruciform Press, 2015.
7. "*450 Sheep Jump to Their Deaths in Turkey*," Yahoo! News, July 8, 2005
8. Anderson, W.R., in his column *Round About Radio*, published in London 1945.
9. Keller, W. Phillip, A Shepherd Looks at Psalm 23, Zondervan, Grand Rapids, MI, 2000.
10. Wight, Fred H., *Manners and Customs of Bible Lands*, Moody Press, Chicago, IL, December, 1953

11. Stilley, Lloyd. *Confidence in Times of Crisis – Psalm 23*, sermon preached on December 4, 2006 at First Baptist Church, Gulf Shores, AL.
12. Murphy, Kelly J. *Commentary on Psalm 23*, The Working Preacher, Luther Seminary, April 17, 2016. Retrieved from www.workingpreacher.org.
13. Schoenian, Susan. *Sheep 201: A Beginner's Guide to Raising Sheep*, 2011. Retrieved from http://www.sheep101.info/201/behavior.html.

Bible References

Unless otherwise noted, all scripture quotations are taken from the (NIV) The New International Version of the Bible. Biblica, Inc., a division of the International Bible Society, Colorado Springs, CO, 2011.

Scripture quotations marked (CEV) are taken from the Contemporary English Version of the Bible, © 1995 by American Bible Society.

Scripture quotations marked (CBV) are taken from the Cloverdale Bible, 1535. Public Domain.

Scripture quotations marked (JCB) are taken from The Complete Jewish Bible, Jewish New Testament Publications, Clarksville, MD, 1998.

Scripture quotations marked (GBV) are taken from The Geneva Bible, England, 1599. Public Domain

Scripture quotations marked (DRA) are taken from the Douay-Rheims Bible, 1899 American Edition. Public Domain

Scripture quotations marked (KJV) are taken from the Authorized King James Bible, 1611. Public Domain

Scripture quotations marked (NKJV) are taken from The New King James Version, Copyright © 1982 by Thomas Nelson.

Scripture quotations marked (ERV) are taken from Easy-to-Read Version of the Bible League International, 2006.

Scripture quotations marked (NRSV) are taken from the New Revised Standard Version Bible, The Division of Christian Education of the National Council of the Churches of Christ in the United States of America, 1989.

Scripture quotations marked (TLB) are taken from The Living Bible by Tyndale House Foundation. Tyndale House Publishers Inc., Carol Stream, IL, 1971.

Scripture quotations marked (NLT) are taken from New Living Translation by Tyndale House Foundation. Tyndale House Publishers Inc., Carol Stream, IL, 2015.

Scripture quotations marked (MSG) are taken from The Message Paraphrase of the Bible. by Eugene H. Peterson, 2002.

Printed in the United States
By Bookmasters